ditch the FEAR

Just Write It!

THE NO-EXCUSES POWER PLAN TO START YOUR FIRST BOOK

Alexa Bigwarfe

Published by Kat Biggie Press.
Columbia, SC 29229
http://katbiggiepress.com

Cover design by Michelle Fairbanks
This book created by licensing the Quick Wins Workbook System by Impact Stars, LLC www.impactstars.com/quick-wins
Interior customized and prepared by Write.Publish.Sell
www.writepublishsell.co
Custom printing by Vervante www.vervante.com

ISBN-13: 978-0-9994377-6-6
Library of Congress Control Number: 2017916001
First Edition: November 2017

10 9 8 7 6 5 4 3 2 1

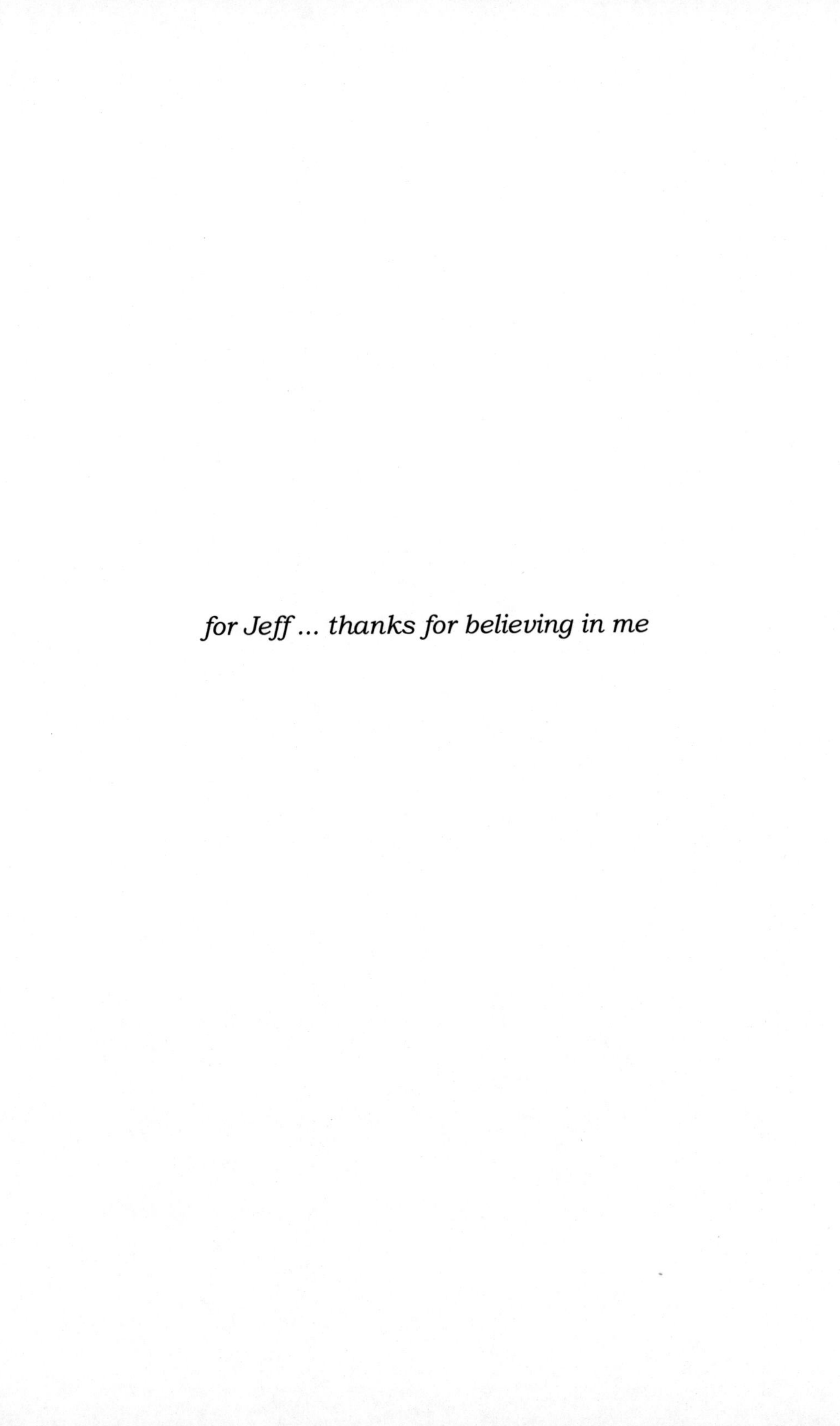

for Jeff ... thanks for believing in me

INTRODUCTION

Why write a book?

I'm sure you've heard the statistics ... more than 80% of the population wants to write a book. But guess what? Only less than 2% of people will actually do it.

Why is this?

Well, for starters, we're busy. Is that the excuse you've been allowing to keep you from achieving your goal?

Or how about the mindset issues that plague us from moving forward? These are huge. I'm not good enough. I'm not smart enough. I don't know enough.

Or maybe you just don't really understand the big picture of what can come to your business from writing a book. I have several testimonies from successful entrepreneurs who are going to tell you exactly what a book can do to move your business forward. But it's up to you to get yourself there and decide you are ready to put forth the time, energy, and money to make this actually happen.

Welcome to your NO EXCUSES guide to getting your book written. I am going to ask you to do a lot of things in this book. This is not a "read it and put it aside" book. This is an action oriented power plan - filled with information and implementation steps. So if you're ready to actually do this, you're going to have to ditch the fear, ditch the excuses, and remove sayings like, "I'm just too busy" from your vocabulary.

If you've chosen to write a book to build your business, I have some fantastic news for you. You probably already have a lot of your content written! Our goal is going to be to find that content and put it to use so that you're not spending time re-creating. And even if you haven't written it down someplace, there's a good chance you've spoken it - on a video, a Facebook live, a podcast interview.

Let's talk about expectations. This is NOT a write your book in 90 days plan. Although for some of you, it may be possible to get it done in that amount of time, or shorter if you commit to it. You'll read in some of the featured stories about women who actually did write their book in a month. If this is your goal, I fully believe that you can do it, especially with the right support team of experts behind you. But with this plan, I encourage you to work through the planning steps and set up those time-lines based on what YOU can realistically achieve.

This is *definitely* not a *publish* your book in 90 days. In fact, we're not going to cover publishing really at all. I do provide some time-lines and some things for you to consider, but for this book, we're focusing on getting the content together and written. I encourage my clients to allow for a solid six months post writing the book for publication, if you want to do a noteworthy book launch.

Throughout this power plan, you will find a page or two about the topic at hand, some implementation steps, and a real-life example of a busy entrepreneur who exemplifies the topic at hand or overcame any associated barrier to get her book done. It is my hope that these stories will resonate with you and show you that this is possible, even if you feel like the odds are against you.

A daily and weekly "planner" is included in the last portion of the book. This is to keep you on track with your daily and weekly book goals and hold you accountable. It's been shown that setting daily, weekly, and monthly intentions can really make a difference in your success. So, if you want to use it to keep your mindset on track, please do so!

I believe in you. I know it can be done. When I decided to write and publish my first book, I had 3 children under the age of six. Probably not the ideal time to write my first book, but it was something I needed to do. If you have a high level of commitment to your book project, you'll make it happen. Just like everything else you want in life.

Are you ready to do this? We are in it together!

Let's write!

Alexa

Alexa Bigwarfe
CEO & Founder,
Kat Biggie Press & Write.Publish.Sell

The World needs your message, so get out of your own way!

WARNING.

THIS IS NO ORDINARY PLAN. IT IS THE ASS-KICKERY YOU NEED WHEN YOU WANT TO GIVE UP.

A book can revolutionize your business in ways you never dreamed. Therefore, this plan is sacred space reserved for the lovely ones who dream big and get it done. Invest in yourself and your journey. This plan is a commitment to yourself.

so be careful

It isn't for excuse-makers or blamers. If that's you, there is nothing for you here.

Ready? Let's do this!

In The Beginning

where to start...

You probably have a million ideas but simply have no idea HOW to start. That's the point of this book - to move you through simple strategies to get going and stay on it.

The question I hear often is: *Should I even write a book? Well...*

If you want to do any of the following, then the answer to the book question is emphatically YES!!!

1. Launch a speaking career. Sometimes this will happen simply BECAUSE of a book, as we'll see in the following example with Claire Diaz-Ortiz.
2. Build credibility in your field.
3. Open a new entry point into your sales funnel. What does this even mean? You can offer your book as a free or low-cost entry point into your business. If you're a coach and concerned people aren't ready to invest in your higher cost services, a low-cost book is a great way for people to learn more about you and gain trust in you.
4. Create passive revenue streams.

There are many other reasons, but these are four of the biggest for entrepreneurs.

We're going to start with some mindset work, so that you can move past the fears you may have.

"Unintentional Speaking Career" Writer

claire diaz-ortiz

AUTHOR, SPEAKER, SILICONE VALLEY INNOVATOR

"I didn't understand the extent to which speaking would become a full-time career for a number of years as a result of writing books."

Claire Diaz-Ortiz (@claire) is an author, speaker and Silicon Valley innovator who was an early employee at Twitter. Named one of the 100 Most Creative People in Business by Fast Company, she holds an MBA and other degrees from Stanford and Oxford and has been featured widely in print and broadcast media. She writes a popular business blog at ClaireDiazOrtiz.com and is the award-winning author of eight books that have been published in more than a dozen countries.

https://www.facebook.com/clairediazortizpublic/
http://clairediazortiz.com

Writing a book is going to give you authority and that's why this is such an essential step in growing your business. I struggled with time, as we all do, but what helped me beyond my fear of the time issue was to think out side of the box. I usually try to just knock out a really crappy first draft all over a short period of time, like a two week retreat. Then I can take time to do a careful editing and revision process within my normal work time. For two of my books, I actually took a cruise to get uninterrupted writing time. If you've been on a cruise, you know that internet is costly and you can shut yourself off from the world.

If speaking is something you have on your bucket list, writing a book is a must-do. The power of authority generated from being an author certainly took me by surprise.

PUBLISHING STORY

When Claire started writing her first book, published in 2010, her goal was just to be published. The book didn't have a whole lot to do with her business, but it was a first step in the publishing process. She learned everything about what it meant to have an agent and get published. She was totally unprepared for the solid speaking career that would follow.

So don't be afraid to think big, think outside of the box, and embrace the amazingness that is headed your way!

MINDSET

fight the fear

I am not a mindset coach, but I DO know there are a lot of mindset issues that can negatively impact you when you set out to write a book. We have so many limiting beliefs, so many fears, so many internal blocks that can really slow us down from achieving our goal of JUST WRITING IT!

Mindset issues are so powerful and can stop us right in our tracks. A lot of the issues center around fear. Yep. We're afraid no one will buy our book, or it will be stupid, or it will get bad reviews... or even worse, WHO AM I to call myself the expert on this topic? Good ole imposter syndrome!

If you have these thoughts, you are not alone. Many of the very successful and confident authors I interviewed faced the same issues! That's why we're starting the book with a good ole lesson on mindset. Let's slay that stupid Fear Beast.

If you're going to be a successful author, you have to BELIEVE you are a successful author. So I want you start by writing your fears and limiting beliefs about your book.

Be brave enough to act in spite of the fear being there.
~ Jennifer Blanchard

dear diary
I SET MYSELF FREE.

Give yourself five minutes to write down all the negative thoughts, fears, worries, and limiting beliefs bottled up inside you related to writing a book. Release them onto this page, so you feel liberated from carrying them around.

"I was more nervous about what would friends and family think. I thought would they say things like 'when did she become a writer?' or 'there is no way she wrote that book'. I definitely had to work through some mindset issues around that."
~ Stacy Tuschl

permission
I BELIEVE IN MYSELF.

If you suffer from imposter syndrome, (meaning, you believe you're not enough of an authority on the subject to write a book about it) you must squash those thoughts immediately. You ARE the expert, and you have a lot to offer the world. Jot down a few thoughts on why YOUR perspective makes you the right person to provide the key messages that you want to share through your book.

____

____

____

____

____

____

____

____

____

____

I give myself permission to believe in myself as a writer!

Date: __/__/____

OVERCOMING SELF-DOUBT

laura jack

GRIEF RECOVERY SPECIALIST

"Write a book from your heart that is authentically you."

Laura is the author of #1 International Best Seller, *The Compassion Code: How to say the right thing when the wrong thing happens*. She teaches compassionate communication and how we can relate to one another more effectively during the challenging moments in life. Using practices of self-care and self-love, she helps people rediscover their light after loss.

My mission in life is not merely to survive, but to thrive; and to do so with some passion, some compassion, some humor, and some style. ~ Maya Angelou

www.facebook.com/groups/theArmyofCompassion

laurajack.com

I wasn't sure if I knew enough. I doubted myself and feared I would be judged for my opinions and perspective. I really didn't have any idea how much time or money it would cost, but I wasn't concerned about that as much.

PUBLISHING STORY

Laura Jack wrote *The Compassion Code: How to say the right thing when the wrong thing happens* as a response to all the people she encountered who struggled with having healthy, compassionate communication when others were grieving or going through challenging times. Her biggest goal was to get her message out to a larger audience so that she could build an "army of compassion"; a group of people who felt more confident supporting others without burning themselves out.

Since publishing, Laura has already noticed an increase in the number of people who would like to interview her on podcasts and radio shows. She anticipates more paid speaking engagements. She has also been asked to write curriculum based on her book for several businesses.

Had Laura stayed stuck in her fears that she didn't know enough on the topic or continued to worry about the way others would respond to her opinions on certain topics, this book would have never made it into the world, and her coaching business would not be growing at the rate it is now.

affirmations

SAY IT EVERYDAY & IT WILL BE.

If only it were as easy as just deciding you're over your self-doubt and moving on to writing a best-selling book! While I don't have all the answers to fixing deep rooted issues, I have some simple exercises that should, at a minimum, help you quiet the disruptive and harmful thoughts. You can never underestimate the impact of positive affirmations.

What is an affirmation? It is a short and powerful statement that helps you train your mind and believe in the potential of our action.

Use positive affirmations to help conquer your fears. I want you to take all of those limiting beliefs and fears you wrote on the first page and turn each into a positive affirmation.

Example: if your fear is: "I can't write a book because I'm not a good writer." You'll turn that into an affirmation like: "I am an expert in my field and I have important information to share with my audience."

"No one will read my book." Turn that into: "There are people who desperately need my book."

And so forth. Remember, you ARE a writer. Add that one to your list and repeat daily!

my writer affirmations

Let's put it into action. In the lines below, write out one fear and then on the line under it, flip that fear into a positive, like the examples I just gave you.

Fear: ____

____

Affirmation: ____

____

Fear: ____

____

Affirmation: ____

____

Fear: ____

____

Affirmation: ____

____

You've got this!

For more resources on Mindset and Writer Affirmations, visit writepublishsell.co/mindset

Visualize

Know Your Why

If you're going to write a book, you're committing time, resources, emotions, and more to a massive endeavor. It can be one of the best things you ever do, but it can also be one of the most challenging. It's important to know your WHY. What is it that you hope to gain from writing your book? How will it change your life or your business? WHY do you want to write this book? What is it going to do for you? WHO is it going to serve? How will it change your life? When things get rough, find refuge here. Come to this page to remember why you're doing this and center yourself.

____

____

____

____

____

____

____

____

____

The Big Picture

growing my biz... with a book

Yes, many of us have big dreams of being a published author. But beyond being able to say, "I'm an author" - do you really see the big picture of what a book can do for your business?

First, let's set one expectation straight right away. You are probably *not* going to get rich from book sales. You might, it's not impossible. Certainly big name entrepreneurs are making a pretty nice mint from their book sales. But lets look at some of the ways a book can directly impact your business, from the outset.

1. Do you dream of being a speaker? A book is considered a weed-out requirement for many events. And guess what? Many speaking engagements at large events pay a lot of cash!
2. New clients - and more higher end clients at that!
3. New income streams - consider how you can now use your book as a key part of your sales funnel. The options are limitless with this option! And what about the option of creating a course from your book? The sky is the limit.

"BUILD MY BUSINESS WITH A BOOK" WRITER

dana malstaff

ENTREPRENEUR, FOUNDER OF BOSS-MOMS

"I realized that the people who were showing interest in the book as I was beginning to promote it were people that I could also help in my business."

Dana is a mother, author, business & content strategist, coach, podcaster, and blind spot reducer. Dana is the author of *Boss Mom: The Ultimate Guide to Raising a Business & Nurturing Your Family Like a Pro*, and the founder of the Boss Mom Movement. She serves Boss Moms who yearn for more time and less guilt when it comes to building their business and raising their family, by providing the tools they need to get more out of their content and business, without sacrificing their family goals.

Ah, but a man's [or woman's] reach should exceed his grasp, Or what's a heaven for? – Robert Browning

https://www.facebook.com/BossMomDana/

boss-mom.com

I had always wanted to write a book and was encouraged by a book coach to write a book to help grow my business. I envisioned writing a business book for female entrepreneurs, but when I did my mind map for my outline, what I saw actually through was the mom guilt associated with building a business while raising my family. When I discovered it was a MOM thing, I wondered if it would be a mom book, not just a business book. As I mapped it out, I saw the two were definitely intertwined - the difficulties of growing a family and a business. I also realized that the people who were showing interest in the book as I was beginning to promote it were people that I could also help in my business.

I realized this was something. So I geared my book marketing tactics around also growing this target audience of moms who might be struggling as they raise their families and their businesses at the same time. The Boss-Mom movement was born.

PUBLISHING STORY

Dana always knew she wanted to write a book. Her mom is a writer, her dad published his first book when she was in 6th grade. It was a huge bucket list item for her. While she was still working in corporate America, she and her husband were sitting around a campfire and started writing a book about how to move forward in your career.

They were brainstorming it and she eventually wrote 3-4 chapters, but never finished it. Not long after that, Dana quit her job and started her own business. The idea to write a book still stayed with her, and about a year after starting her business, she met a book coach at a Mastermind in San Diego. With his encouragement, Dana thought it was the right time to move forward with her book.

Dana's husband actually thought it was a bad idea at the time. He thought it was a deviation from her business goals and believed she should focus on other areas of development in her business. He was concerned, but Dana told him that it was something that she just needed to do. At the time, it was probably more a passion project, even though she believed it was a strategic business move. She had no idea how much writing that first book would actually change and define her business.

The idea of doing a book was always a passion for Dana, she also realized a book could be leveraged. Dana made the connection that the message she was bringing forward in her book was a business idea in itself and had a massive potential for women that she could actually help in her business. And that's when all the things started coming together and she realized that *Boss Mom* was not just going to be a book, but it would be the entire brand and focus of her business.

The whole book writing process helped clarify her brand. And because it helped clarify her brand, she was able to talk about it more clearly, have something tangible to help her get more visibility on podcasts and other places, and overall help her lay out the strategy for her business.

Dana mentioned that this all came about from her mind mapping session which turned into more of a therapy session as she became aware of what she really wanted to share with people and wanted her message to include. This type of clarity comes from having a well-defined vision for your book. The mind map and outline are tremendous elements of this step. We'll cover these in the next section: Tools.

TOOLS

getting started

You'll probably be working on mindset issues throughout the entire process. As stress kicks in, limitations on your time, and all the other things that happen in life, you may start to doubt whether or not you can do this. But I promise you can.

Once we've started conquering those mindset issues, what are the mechanics you need to get moving forward?

The simple answer is the title of this book: Just Write It!

Obviously, there is more to it than that, or everyone would write a book, right? You can write when you have the proper tools in your toolbox.

This is the NO-EXCUSES, NO-FEAR plan, and these are the tools you are going to need:

1. Commitment and dedicated writing time
2. SMART goals
3. A "living" outline - including mind mapping
4. Research and data based on your outline
5. The belief that your book is needed
6. A solid support network

commit to it!

Writing Is Like Exercise

Just as you would exercise your muscles for 15-30 minutes daily to stay in shape, you need to exercise your writing muscle as well. You need to commit to 15-30 minutes of writing at least five days a week. We can re-arrange that model if you are a time-blocker. For example, if you know you can't write 5 days a week, then schedule out larger blocks of time on fewer days. So, 60 minutes a day 3 times a week. The schedule is not nearly as important as committing to a certain number of days per week and a certain amount of time. Consider it will probably take about 30 minutes to write 500 words. Your book will probably average around 30,000 words. That means you need to plan for sixty 30-minute blocks of time to complete the first draft of a your book.

Determining Your Time-line

I recommend you pick a goal launch date for your book. We'll talk about goal setting a little later, but having a set goal date of publication will really help you stay on track. A launch day should be on a Tuesday, Wednesday, or Thursday for the best success rates. You probably do NOT want to launch around Black Friday or Christmas, simply because you will be competing with every other business under the sun. Other than that, there are no real rules for your launch, other than to make sure it is enough time to get everything done well. If your community is moms, perhaps a launch around Mother's Day makes sense, as an example.

When considering the launch day, think about the following elements to help you determine a rough time frame. (This is for example purposes only. Depending on the nature of your book, it can be significantly shorter, or significantly longer. However, if you want to do the editing and publication preparation stages faster than this, you will usually have to pay a rush fee. And why rush your book - take the time to do it right.)

- Time required for writing an approximatley 30,000 word book - approximately 30 hours
- Revisions / input and feedback from Beta Readers - 2-4 weeks
- Editing - up to a month
- Formatting/layout/ebook conversion/publication preparation - up to a month
- Proper marketing and launch preparation (should be ongoing) - at least 2-3 months, but this will be concurrent with the other activities

So... depending on how much time you have available to write the first draft, you can pick a reasonable launch time frame. Obviously, the more time a week you can commit to writing, the better. If you commit 5 hours/week, it will take approximately 6 weeks to write. Then you'll need to add 3 months for the publication preparation.

MAKE YOUR COMMITMENT.

I will commit to writing _________/hours per week.
It will take ____________ weeks for me to finish my draft.
__________ + 3-6 months publication/marketing = ________ months required.
My estimated launch/publication date will be:
____

BUT I'M TOO BUSY.

If talking about the amount of time required just freaked you out, relax. The good news is, you can hire help for all of those things, with exception to the words that you actually want to write. You'll hire pros to edit, layout, prepare for publication, market for you, etc.

We are all busy. This is the NO EXCUSES plan. If you're starting out of the gate with "I'm too busy" you might need to just hang up your dreams of writing a book.

OR... you can commit to making writing a priority and finding the time.

Think of the things you do every day that are not moving your toward your book goal. This includes watching television, chatting on the telephone, Facebooking or otherwise scrolling through social media in a non productive manner, and so forth. Ditch these and write during this time instead!

NO-EXCUSES, FOCUSED WRITER

kelsey humphreys

ENTREPRENEUR, SPEAKER, AUTHOR

"Writing a book is a huge commitment so I had to let other things go like social life, TV, cleaning my house!"

Kelsey is a personal branding strategist on a mission to break down "success for the rest of us." She is the host and producer of The Pursuit, an in-person, video talk show and audio podcast, where she interviews today's most influential entrepreneurs and celebrities. She is the author of Amazon Entrepreneurship #1 bestseller *Go Solo* and a regular conference speaker and emcee. Oh and she is building her media empire as a wife and mom in suburbia, Oklahoma.

Fortune favors the bold {who work their hiney off}.

http://facebook.com/kelseyhumphreys
kelseyhumphreys.com

WORDS OF WISDOM
KELSEY HUMPHREYS

Don't try and bust out a great book in a month. Really take your time and make it awesome. Don't try to do it all yourself, hire a designer and editor, ask colleagues and clients for early feedback. Then, let perfectionism go and allow yourself to make the book a priority and let other things in your life slide for a while as you sprint to your book finish line.

Also, I pushed past all my self-doubt with public deadlines and sharing about the book even though I was scared. I asked friends and family to proof it, promote it, etc even though that felt awkward because they're not my target audience. But getting them involved really helped keep me on track.

PUBLISHING STORY

Kelsey has always had big goals for her business. She started building her brand while she was still employed full-time in corporate America. Once she had her own company, she decided she needed a book to launch her speaking career. She knew a book would give her the credibility to start speaking and writing for large websites like Entrepreneur.

Despite having a *newborn*, Kelsey committed herself to finishing her book. She would write in spurts while the baby slept. Kelsey also admits that since writing a book is such a huge commitment, she had to let other things go; like social life, TV, cleaning her house!

If you want it badly enough, and you are committed to making it happen, you *will* find the time.

You've already listed out the things you do that take up your time. We've worked through how much time you NEED to write your book. Now, let's schedule dedicated writing time!

Implementation step:

Go through your calendar and identify daily and weekly blocks in your calendar where you will write.

Every. Day. Or you can batch like you might with blogging or time spent working in your business. Just make sure you have created some space in your schedule. This could be early morning, late night, or even on the weekends, your choice, but ***commit to the time.***

Treat these like appointments that are just as important as any other business related deadline/ appointment.

Bring Your Network On Board Early

A great way to hold yourself accountable is to announce to the world that you are working on a book. Once other people know that you're working on this project, they will start to ask you about it. This alone is enough motivation to keep on track and to make the writing a priority.

I encourage my clients to set up a launch team from very early on in the process. It may be scary to think about sharing details of your book when you have just started writing, but it's amazing how much support you can get from a launch team, which will keep you motivated. The launch team is comprised of the people that will be your biggest cheerleaders throughout the process. You can create a community (like a group on Facebook, or a special email list) where you keep them updated on your progress. Let them be part of the process—they can help you pick your title, your cover design, encourage you when you're feeling stressed, help you brainstorm when you feel stuck, answer polls and surveys when you need input or feedback. They'll love being a part of your book launch!

TIME IS NOT AN EXCUSE

YOU DON'T HAVE TO SEE THE WHOLE STAIRCASE

JUST TAKE THE FIRST STEP.

Yesterday is gone. Tomorrow has not yet come. We have only today. Let us begin.

- MOTHER THERESA -

my crazy big goal (CBG)

WHAT DO I WANT?

You're committed, you have a time line, you've kicked some of your mindset fears in the face, it's time to make sure your goals are spot on. You are an entrepreneur. The concept of setting goals is not new to you. You KNOW that if you want to accomplish something, you have to be intentional. And part of being intentional is setting your overarching goal with many small achievable goals to get you there.

Publish my book. That is a crazy big goal! We won't achieve this goal in 90 days but I want you to write it on the line below anyway. Because you're committed!

My crazy big goal is to:

____

(write: PUBLISH MY BOOK).

Imagine achieving this goal of publishing your book six months to one year from now. What do you need to do in the next 90 days so you can position yourself to achieve your CBG? Refer back to the rough time line I sketched out for you, and set your specific mini goals based on that.

Specific, Measurable, Action-Oriented, Realistic & Time-Bound.

I provided you some general time frames for how long it will take you to write a draft, based on just sitting down to WRITE, but there is often more to that. There may be some other tasks you need to do to complete your first draft (and estimated time frames to complete):

1. Outline - anywhere from 1 hour to 1 week depending on how detailed you go

2. Research and gather data - this depends on how heavily your book relies on research. When I wrote my first book, *Lose the Cape: Realities for Busy Modern Moms and Strategies to Survive*, my co-author and I spent months collecting data from doctors, psychologists, and parenting experts. However, your book may be based primarily on your knowledge and experience and only require a few hours of extra research.

3. Conduct interviews if needed - one of our featured writers in this book, Suzanne Brown, spent three years interviewing subjects for her book. For this book, I was able to really shorten the interview time down to two weeks by providing a form with specific questions to answer. I also voxered with a few people to clarify, but the interview time was not intense at all.

Think about how long each of those steps might take, and set a goal deadline for each of those steps for the next twelve weeks.

Try your best to be realistic about these goals, but also create some sort of sense of urgency. The longer you push off the writing, the longer it will take you to publish your book.

Break those SMART goals down into daily and weekly chunks.

For example, I will complete my Outline by the end of week one.

I will write _______ words per week so that I can complete my first draft by _____ (date).

I will complete my first draft by ________(date) so I can get my book to the editor by _____________ (date).

Or perhaps each week is a chapter. Your SMART goal will read something like: Chapter 1 - complete chapter draft by Week 2 (date). You can further break those down into smaller goals. For Chapter 1, I need to research topics x,y,z by _____________(date).

chunk it up

BREAK IT DOWN

Use this space to write out some of your specific goals for the next 12 weeks.

We can't become what we need to be by remaining where we are.

~ Oprah Winfrey

You aren't writing a college thesis paper, so don't freak out about the word *outline*. Consider it a road map to help keep you on track with the book. It is amazing how easily you can get sidetracked with all the different knowledge that you have - the good news is, you can write MULTIPLE books. But stay on track and keep to one message.

In Dana Malstaff's publishing story, she mentioned the use of a mind map. A mind map is a really fun process to help the outlining seem less daunting. You can draw your mind map on a big piece of paper, on a white board or chalkboard, on the wall, wherever.

The concept is simple. You put your main topic idea in the center of the page. Then you just start writing "offshoots" of things that you think of - your key ideas. As you write these ideas, more ideas will pop into your mind. Keep writing and writing as long as the ideas flow into your mind.

For example, if you're writing a book about starting a blog. In the center of your page, you'll write:

"how to start a blog"

From there just let the ideas flow. When I think of things someone starting a blog would need to know, I think about hosting and domains, what they are, how to get one, different platforms you might blog on, how to pick a theme and set up your theme, plugins and widgets - what you need and how you get them, and so on and so forth.

Every time you write one thing, more items will pop in your mind. Just keep branching off and writing more and more. Fill the page. Don't stop until you feel like you have all of the key points addressed.

A simple version of the mind map will look something like this, but probably not as neat! Get all the ideas on the paper and don't worry about keeping it pretty!

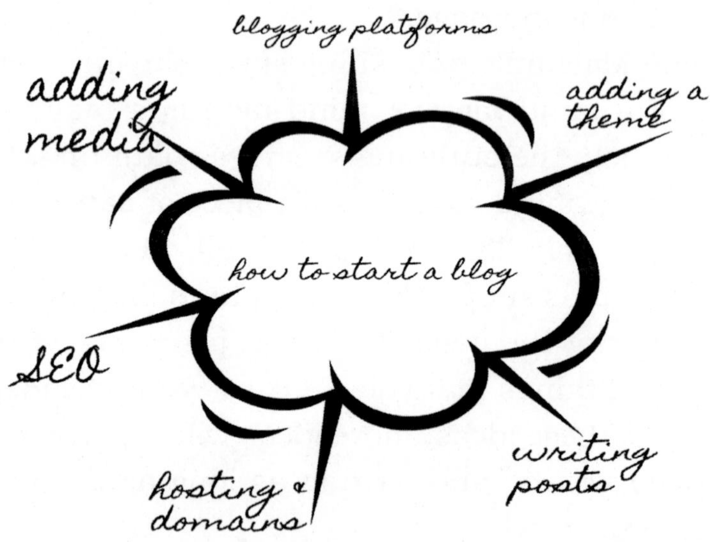

Like Dana, you may find that your mind map leads you to places you didn't know you wanted to go, and that's okay! Go with what comes easiest and most naturally to you.

The next step is to start organizing the ideas in

similar subject groups. Start with the main point and list everything that you think would fall under that topic area. This will form your very basic framework of your outline. Wasn't that fun?

Keep your outline simple: focus on the MAJOR points you want to make in your book. I'll give another example. If you're writing about growing your Facebook page, your major topics might look something like this:

- different types of posts (memes, questions...)
- Using Facebook Live
- How to create posts people want to share
- Inviting people to like your page

... and so forth. Brainstorm the key ideas, and then later you can take those and fill in the details.

Use a "working outline" that you can tailor along the way. You can always change the outline as you go, but it's important to have something to keep you focused. Your road map is key.

As soon as I decided I wanted to write a book, I started on the outline, I gave myself daily goals for how much to write, and then I just got started! ~ *Samantha Munoz*

research & data

Fill In the Gaps

A note about research and writing your first draft: research is important, but don't let it slow you down when writing your first draft, unless it is essential to what you are writing. When you are on a roll with ideas and thoughts, you do not want to disrupt that just to collect the data to back up your point. If you do need to add data or research, highlight that area and come back to it later. Kind of like you should never wake a sleeping baby, never interrupt a good stream of words flowing onto the page.

If you're lucky, you won't have to do a huge amount of research and data collection. As the expert in your field and on your topic, I imagine much of the information you are going to share is based on your own experiences and knowledge... maybe!

But what if you need some data to back up your information? My friend and client, Tonya Rineer, author of *The Mindset Switch*, wanted to make sure the information on why we make the decisions that we do as entrepreneurs was backed by scientific data on the way the brain is programmed. So, while she is able to write the majority of the content from her own knowledge and experience, we had to plan for some time to collect the other data to back up her statements and conclusions.

“Collect All the Data!” Writer

suzanne brown

EXPERT ON AND ADVOCATE FOR PROFESSIONAL PART-TIME WORKING MOMS

“I wanted to use the book to set me up as an expert. Part of what I want to do in my business is offer consulting to businesses related to this topic and to speak at large company events and industry conferences. This book helps set me up as that expert.”

Suzanne is a strategic marketing and business consultant, TEDx speaker, and author of *Mompowerment: Insights from Successful Professional Part-time Working Moms Who Balance Career and Family.* She empowers moms to think differently about their career approach and provides guidance on work-life balance. She lives in Austin, TX with her husband and two young boys.

“In my business...everything is a baby step to something else.”

www.facebook.com/mompowerment
www.mompowerment.com

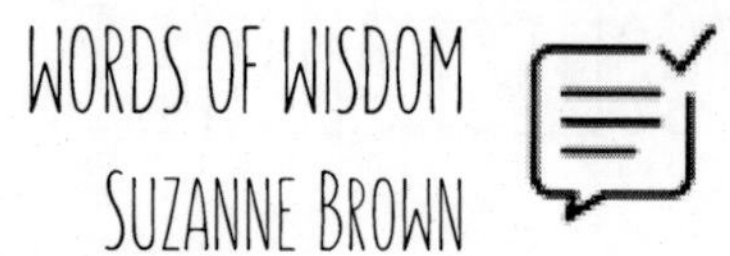

In order to really have the best insight into what the world really looks like for part-time working moms required a lot of interviewing and data collection. I put in 3 years of research (granted, I was working part-time during that).

Time was a struggle. As a part-time strategic marketing and business consultant, I have clients to support and deadlines to meet as well as continue to build a pipeline of business. Mix into that interviewing other professional part-time working moms for the book + writing the book and still being the primary caregiver for my children while trying to maintain a strong marriage, do volunteer work, etc. It comes down to it's a lot.

The whole process of publishing a book is a lot more complicated than I had anticipated. I am thankful I had Alexa as a guide.

My advice is to know why you want to write a book and make sure that your book actually meets that business or personal need. Don't write a book because everyone else in your industry is writing a book.

PUBLISHING STORY

Suzanne had two purposes with writing her book.

1. The book will help spread the word to working moms so they have a one-stop resource to help them with a transition to a professional part-time role and to help with work-life balance.

2. She wanted to use the book to set herself up as an

expert for her business. Part of what she wants to do in her business is offer consulting to businesses related to this topic and to speak at large company events and industry conferences. This book gives her the credibility to do so. You don't need a book to be an expert, but it does help.

Suzanne also recognized the value of having a book as another revenue stream. Overall, the book fits nicely into her strategy.

believe

Your Message is Needed

You can have all the research and data in the world, but if you don't believe that the world needs your message and there's an important place for your information, it's going to be very difficult to stay committed to your project.

Hopefully the stories shared have given you a belief that a book is an important addition to "tools" you need in your toolbox to grow your business to really high places. But perhaps you don't realize that there is someone out there searching for the information that you have to provide.

If your business centers around helping others, particularly in an advocacy way, there are so many people that will benefit from your message. Writing a book can not only provide that help and support, it can help move you forward in advocacy.

Amie Lands is a wonderful example of this. She knew she had to write her book because it was the book she could not find when she needed it most. Amie's story is very touching and serves a very large and important service. While your story may be completely different, the point to take away is that there is always someone in need of the information that YOU know.

But your book doesn't have to contain a life-altering message to be needed. Believe in your message!

"Fill a Void" Writer

amie lands

TEACHER, ADVOCATE, NONPROFIT FOUNDER

"Publishing these books propelled me into more advocacy work. I want this message to spread internationally."

Amie Lands is a wife, mother, teacher and author. She is the proud founder of The Ruthie Lou Foundation and a Certified Grief Recovery Specialist®. Her most sacred role in life is being "mama" to 3 beautiful children: her daughter, who she held for 33 days, and her two sons who she has the privilege to watch grow.

What I need is the dandelion in the spring. The bright yellow that means rebirth instead of destruction. The promise that life can go on, no matter how bad our losses. That it can be good again. — Suzanne Collins

https://www.facebook.com/RuthieLouFoundation/
http://www.ruthieloufoundation.org/

There is someone looking for your book. I wrote Navigating the Unknown *because I couldn't find the exact book I was looking for after my daughter died. I wanted a friend to hold my hand, give me hope that I would survive this loss, while answering the devastating questions I had during that time.* Our Only Time *was inspired by the beautiful care I received during my daughters brief life and after her death. I assumed others received similar care. My hope is that through this book, health professionals can best support parents to have the least amount of regret when leaving the hospital without their baby.*

Believing in the magnitude of this message helped me ignore my fears. The fear is still there everyday; rejection, judgment, humiliation, but I want to help families. This matter is life and death to me. If a family does not have support, this loss will ruin the remainder of their life and that is unacceptable to me. This is my passion, this is my purpose. I feel the fear and do it anyway.

Amie's advice: *Just start writing! Let your words just flow. Give yourself plenty of time for the publishing side if you're self publishing.*

PUBLISHING STORY

When Amie learned that her daughter would not survive, writing became her emotional outlet, to process her emotions and to educate others on the grieving process.

This has become her passion and calling: to write, to educate, and to advocate for bereaved families. Through grief work, soul searching and heart healing, joy has found it's way into Amie's life once again.

Amie wrote *Navigating the Unknown* December 2015-July 2016 and it published in January 2017. As she moved forward with the process, both time and money were legitimate fears. Amie was pregnant and had a toddler at home when she wrote *Navigating the Unknown*, so she had more time available, than if she'd been working full time, but when she started the second book, *Our Only Time,* she had two young children and a full time day job to tend to! She had to be creative with her time. Early mornings before work, late nights after kid's bedtimes and Saturday mornings were her favorite times to write, promote and work on all things related to the books.

Financially, she and her husband agreed that the investment was worth it. They wanted the book to be taken seriously, therefore, they knew they needed to hire professional help for the cover, editing, interior design and the final publishing. And she believe that if the book helped even ONE FAMILY to feel less alone, then all the time and money spent creating the book was worth it.

Amie admits that publishing these books propelled her into more advocacy work. The Ruthie Lou Foundation Comfort Boxes are used locally, but she want this message to spread internationally. Releasing the books inspired her to do more, to speak more, to write more and to reach out to other professionals within the health care field.

Your story is needed too. There is someone who needs the skills and lessons you can teach, the resources you can provide. Believe it and *Just Write It!*

on rough days

Remember Your Support Network

Your tribe... these are the people who have your back and will support you when you feel like you can't get it all done. This may seem like a strange piece to include, but an accountability partner or partners and/or a group of your inner circle that you know understands how important this goal is to you is HUGE when trying to accomplish a goal as massive as writing a book! Lean on your tribe!

Maybe they'll help brainstorm, or proofread and provide feedback. Maybe they'll take you out of the house if you haven't left in three solid weeks. Whatever their role, it's important to have people that understand the importance of your goal and will stop you from unraveling.

People I consider my tribe and I commit to telling about my project and asking for their support:

____

____

____

____

"Find your tribe. Surround yourself with people who will support you. There will be moments when you lose faith in yourself and your book, these people will lift you up and push you through." ~ Mallika Malhotra

"Use Your Tribe" Writer

herchel scruggs

BLOGGER, AUTHOR, SPEAKER

"My support system kept me going. My tribe assured me that the book would help bloggers that were one to two years into their blogging journey."

Herchel is the mom behind the blog Gym Craft Laundry. Herchel left behind a stressful job, great coworkers, and a hellish commute to pursue life as a work-at-home-mom. Herchel is the author of *Let's Collab*!, the bestselling book for bloggers looking to find their tribes.

You're not going to be great at everything. Surround yourself with people that can compliment you so you can work together and then everybody can be successful.
~ Jonathan Tisch

http://facebook.com/GymCraftLaundry
http://gymcraftlaundry.com

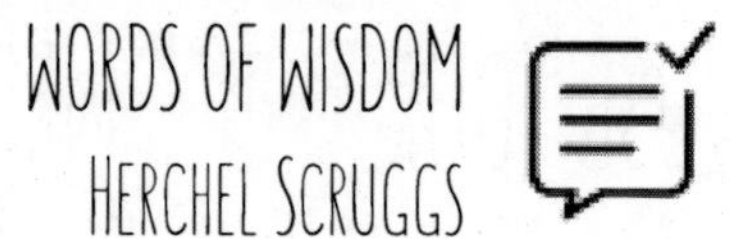

***Let's Collab! Find the blogging tribe that will Skyrocket your Business** was a passion project. It was written to help other bloggers find the same kind of support that my tribe has given to me.*

My book has introduced me to bloggers of all experience levels. I've had a chance to speak at a blogging conference and see first hand how the struggle to find a tribe affects new bloggers.

PUBLISHING STORY

When Herchel set out to write her book, she wasn't sure if the topic would be one that was even needed in the community because of the apparent lack of search traffic on it. After speaking to a group of women that included many that are in her target audience and seeing their reactions as she described what she wanted to write about, she realized that this is a struggle that many bloggers have.

It was still difficult to spend the time, money, and personal investment on a book that she was afraid would not be needed in the marketplace, but her tribe assured her that this was a book needed for bloggers in their first two years of blogging.

Because of the book, Herchel has placed herself as an expert and has started some freelance consulting to help others with their blogs.

How Will I Get It Done & What Will I Write?

use what you have

It's not an uncommon occurrence for me to have a call with a female entrepreneur who absolutely knows that she wants to write a book, completely understands the benefits that come along with writing a book, but doesn't know where to start. She often fears two major things:

1. What will I write about?

and

2. When will I find the time to get this done? (not a surprising fear for a busy entrepreneur!)

The first one is a very common fear, even amongst women who are at the top of their game. Half of the writers who participated in the interviews for this journal expressed that at some point in time they struggled with what they would actually write about. Let's not forget, you may not always feel like you're an expert, but if you're running a business and producing a product or a service, you are an expert in a whole slew of things that others have no idea how to do.

In this section we're gong to cover three areas to help you with the struggles of feeling like an expert and feeling as though you can never find enough time to complete this project. I'm going to show you how:

- Frequently asked questions will guide you to your area of expertise
- Content you already have will save you time

use your expertise

I AM THE EXPERT.

You're running a business, so, odds are, you are asked the same questions repeatedly. Think about some of these questions you spend countless hours answering in discovery calls, in emails, or in the group you run (if you have one). You probably have even written a ton of content around these questions. Am I right?

If you haven't, this is the perfect opportunity to start collecting data that can be part of this book or a future book. It's brilliant when you think about it. Your client and potential clients, and even others simply interested in your business, are handing you topics for all the content creation you could ever possibly want to write about.

Do a search through your email, questions in your group, and other places you may have answered questions, and write down the most common questions. Do you see a theme? While you are doing this, start creating topic-based files with the questions and your answers. You'll see why in the next section.

Now, use this to your advantage, like Mallika Malhotra. She found she was getting the same questions asked, over and over again. So she decided there was definitely a need for her book. She got to work and published her book eight months later.

"FILL THE GAP" WRITER

mallika malhotra

PHOTOGRAPHER + BRAND STRATEGIST

"Writing a book has shifted my business approach. I not only consider myself a brand photographer but now also an educator, consultant and author."

Mallika is a professional photographer, strategist, educator and author. She is on a mission to empower thousands of woman to be the face of their brand and share their message with confidence. She combines her strategy, storytelling and photography skills to help women move from invisible to impact and emerge as leaders in their industry. Her book *The Brand Photography Playbook* helps her achieve these goals.

The most alluring thing a woman can have is confidence.
- Beyonce

https://www.facebook.com/mikifoto/
www.mikifoto.com

I was asked the same questions repeatedly about brand photography. What is it? Why do I need it for my business? What does it look like? With the rise of online businesses, I thought it would be valuable to share my expertise and photography process. A book was my way to share the power of visual storytelling with more people.

Writing a book has shifted my business approach. I not only consider myself a brand photographer but now also an educator, consultant, and author. I am spending more time teaching and speaking about the topic of brand photography.

My best advice: 1) Hire people to help you! Invest in experts - this will help the book process. 2) Find a support network. I was in a mastermind group that held me accountable with my writing goals. Their support on deadlines and content was amazing. 3) Schedule the time to write into your day. I blocked off two afternoons per week to focus on the book.

PUBLISHING STORY

Mallika had a goal to build confidence and encourage visibility for her target audience. She wanted to present the message that it's not only about creating beautiful photos but the action of sharing your story to inspire and connect with your audience.

Mallika knew there was a need for her book, but she still entered the process sceptically. She was overwhelmed by all of the pieces that she didn't know or understand about publishing, like working with Create Space or other printers/distributors, buying an ISBN number, technical details, like the placement of the Table of Contents page, all the way to proper language on the sales page. (Don't panic about this stuff yet! When the time comes, there are experts - like me - who can help you figure these things out!) Everyday there was a new challenge for her. It was overwhelming but she invested in people who know books, editing and publishing. Mallika says this team was essential in navigating the book journey.

Despite her challenges, publishing a book has been a very positive experience for her business. It opened up doors to speak at summits, podcasts and networking events. She is now able to better position and market myself as an expert. The book has also helped in new collaboration opportunities.

Even though Mallika knew there was a need for her book, she still struggled with mindset issues. She worried that the book already existed and there was no need for her to produce one. This is where I encourage you to trust your gut and to understand that you have a message that is different from the rest of the world. If people didn't need Mallika's knowledge, they wouldn't have continued to ask the questions. Sure, there may be a similar book in existence. Clearly Mallika's clients weren't aware of it. Now she has a product that she can direct them to every time they start asking these questions.

What are some of the most frequently asked questions you get asked?

i am the expert

I AM THE GO-TO PERSON.

Implementation Step:

Pay attention to what people ask you for 3 months. Write them down. Keep a running document with the questions and the answers that you provide them.

MONTH 1 ____________/____

QUESTIONS I AM ASKED

i am the expert

I AM THE GO-TO PERSON.

MONTH 2 ____________/____

QUESTIONS I AM ASKED

i am the expert

I AM THE GO-TO PERSON.

MONTH 3 ______________/_____

QUESTIONS I AM ASKED

re-purpose your content

WHY RECREATE THE WHEEL?

The second fear we're addressing is time. When will I ever find the time to get this book written? It's a real struggle. We've talked about how to add it into your schedule and set up dedicated writing times, but there is another solution that will help you write your book faster.

Don't start from ZERO.

You want to know how people pump out a book in a weekend or 30 days? This is how. They use what they have already created.

The simple act of re-purposing content can save you so much time and create a solid base for your book. You've spent months, perhaps years, creating content for your readers on your website, your social media, your email list, or other places. Grab the most relevant content and scoop yourself! This is what Jennifer Blanchard, best selling author and mindset coach, did. Why start from scratch when you already have the makings of a fantastic book?

Implementation Step:

In the previous section, while you were identifying the questions you are asked most frequently, I noted you should start a database of your responses.

Do a search through your email, questions in your group, and other places you may have answered questions, and write down the most common questions. Do you see a theme? While you are doing this, start creating topic-based files with the questions and your answers. You'll see why in the next section.

"We all have a book inside of us and often more than one. Instead of waiting until you are ready to write a book, start writing it now. Even if it is just a Google doc—every time you think of something write it down. It will make the writing process a lot of easier when you have something to work with." ~Stacy Tuschl

"BUILD ON WHAT YOU'VE ALREADY GOT" WRITER

jennifer blanchard
AUTHOR & MINDSET COACH

"I wanted to find another use for a collection of the blog posts I'd written. That's how Butt-In-Chair was born, and my book-writing obsession was started."

Jennifer is a best selling author and a success mindset coach. She's the founder of Dream Life Or Bust, a movement to inspire, motivate, educate and empower multi-passionate writers, artists and creators to build a dream life around all of their passions and interests, so they can have the freedom to live on their terms and never have to choose just one thing.

Decide that what you know is more important than what you have been taught to believe.
-Ralph Waldo Emerson

www.facebook.com/dreamlifeorbust
www.jenniferblanchard.net

My biggest goal was to motivate, inspire and empower other writers to go after their writing dreams.

My books have driven thousands of people to my free Facebook group, gotten me private coaching clients, and introduced thousands of writers to me and my brand.

My best advice: Hire a coach. Don't convince yourself that you can do it on your own the first time. And if you don't hire someone to help you, you may end up putting something out there that isn't the best it could possibly be. Set yourself up for success and get help. At the very least, hire a damn good content editor. And an accountability buddy.

PUBLISHING STORY

Jennifer always knew she was going to be a successful author with hundreds of books under her brand. Publishing the first book was just a step in that direction. She has published numerous books in both the non-fiction and the fiction world. It took only a couple of weeks to write her first book, largely because she relied on content she already had available and because of her comfort with her topic. She was ready to write and get that one published and completely confident in herself to do so. Most of her subsequent nonfiction books have taken less than a month to write as well.

As an expert in her field as a success mind coach, Jennifer relayed that her nonfiction books come easily to her. But she really struggled with her first fiction book, because that is her soul work and the thing she was born to do (write and tell stories). It took her 18 years to write and publish her first novel, which she finally did in 2015. She admits that the struggles there were 99% mindset and fear.

Through the process, one big lesson Jennifer learned is that she didn't need a traditional publisher OR an agent to have the success she was dreaming of. She's totally self-published and an independent author and has sold thousands of books.

How to Use what You've Already Got

Implementation Tip:

Don't sit around waiting for the perfect moment or the perfect content! Use Jennifer's story as an example. She took what she already had, put it into a book, and boom, she was off. If you've spent any time at all blogging, sending emails to your list, answering questions in Facebook groups, going live, or any of those types of scenarios, you have content.

Action Tips:

1. Have some transcribe your Facebook lives, YouTube videos, or other recorded content.

2. Pull together any blog posts, content from Social Media, and emails. Organize by topic and pull the best information from this.

3. Any time you answer questions, respond in a group to a question on a topic of your expertise, or have any opportunity to create content, copy and paste it into a Word or Google Doc on that subject area. When the right time comes, you'll have a whole library of content to pull from.
4. Have you put together a course or courses? Grab any written materials from there, and transcribe any video or audio lessons.

The key is to make the information as fresh and relevant as possible. Do NOT just copy and paste your most popular blog posts into a word document and call it good. While you can use them as a great starting point, be sure to make your book a valuable resource by adding even more to what you already have. But this process can certainly help you get started!

OTHER WAYS TO FIND CONTENT

Tell stories. That is, include anecdotes that will personalize your book for the reader, even if you are not using actual examples of others' experiences. You can use stories to show what is possible in her case, if she follows your advice.

FINAL NOTE ON CONTENT AND TIME

If you are really struggling with time to write your content, you might consider hiring a collaborative writer. Stacy Tuschl did this and it was very helpful to her book.

"CALLING IN THE RESERVES" WRITER

stacy tuschl

HIGH PERFORMANCE COACH & MARKETING STRATEGIST

"I worked with a collaborative writer. She took all of my words, interviewed me for stories, etc. and kept me on track. We discussed deadlines together and made sure we stuck to it. I know having that accountability held me to it."

Stacy is the Best-Selling Author of *Is Your Business Worth Saving?* and the creator of She's Building Her Empire Podcast & Community where she helps purpose-driven women entrepreneurs break through their challenges, operate at their highest potential and create self-sustaining businesses. Stacy is highly passionate about helping women unapologetically be themselves and create a legacy they can be proud of.

"Never be the smartest person in the room."

www.facebook.com/stacytuschl
www.shesbuildingherempire.com

My book has definitely given my business credibility. Writing a book is not a simple task and knowing that you have the discipline to start and finish something like a book definitely adds credibility in my eyes. I also wanted to make sure that I not only wrote a great book, but I launched it in a way that helped my credibility too. Within 24 hours we hit #1 international best seller in many categories.

What helped me move forward was knowing there was more out there. Something bigger. I didn't know what, but I knew it was worth taking that risk and not caring what people thought. I just went for it like I do with anything else. And now that it's done, I know the book has given me many speaking opportunities, podcast interviews, etc, which has ultimately led to more clients.

PUBLISHING STORY

Stacy wanted to share her ups and downs in building her businesses and she knows quite a bit on the topic since she started her first business at the age of 18 in her parents' backyard and turned that company into a 7 figure business she still runs today.

Stacy decided to self-publish her book with the help of a team of experts, including a collaborative writer. She loved being able to control the direction of the book. She used a full team of experts, including a collaborative writer, who got all of the information from Stacy and put the first draft together. Stacy said she made sure the content and stories were 100% her and outsourced the rest, which saved her time and allowed her to continue to focus on her business. She also used a cover designer and professional editor.

All told, it took about a year and a half for her to publish her book. She knew it could have been done faster, but having it done right—a product she was proud of, was far more important to her than having it done quickly.

Stacy's story demonstrates some really relatable situations. She was afraid of what her family and friends would think and worried they might ask: *When did she become a writer?* So she had some mindset issues to work through. But she was committed to getting her book written and knew the benefit would be tremendous to her business.

Stacy also realized the value of trusting other expert freelancers to do the elements that she herself was not an expert in. If you're really nervous about all of the things that go along with writing a book that have nothing to do with writing, don't be! There are plenty of people that can help you through the process, including my company, Write.Publish.Sell.

For more resources on author support services to help you in your book writing journey, visit:

www.writepublishsell.co/services

Other Considerations

it's not just about writing

You probably understand that it's not just about writing, based on the amount of time that we've spent on mindset issues, but there are some other considerations you need to keep in mind on this book writing journey.

In this section we are going to talk about:

- launching a business from a book & unexpected business shifts
- positioning yourself in the market
- self-care through your journey

dream big!

BUSINESS GROWTH IS COMING TO ME.

Give yourself five minutes to write down all the thoughts and dreams you have for what could happen to your business once you've published your book. Dream big!

"My Book Launched My Business" Writer

Samantha Munoz

EXPERT KID'S LIT CURATOR

"I didn't know my business would get to where it is today, but I am so happy it all started with my book."

Samantha is a mother, wife, engineer, bibliophile and avid coffee drinker. She is also the expert kid's lit curator at Addison Reads, author of *The Intentional Bookshelf* and founder of The Intentional Book Club. Sam helps parents as they search for the perfect books for their little ones and helps moms and dads build a library with a purpose. Once a seriously overwhelmed and stressed out parent herself, Sam turns to children's literature for the answers to all of her parenting dilemmas. She loves when it rains because it gives her an excuse to stay inside and read with her daughter!

I am a part of everything that I have read.
- Theodore Roosevelt

https://www.facebook.com/addisonreads/
www.addisonreads.com

WORDS OF WISDOM
SAMANTHA MUNOZ

I decided to write The Intentional Bookshelf *because I had this abstract concept and method for curating books that I wanted to solidify and teach to people. Ultimately, I found that writing a book would be the most effective way to help parents learn this concept by providing actionable steps, and the chance to come back to the text again and again. My biggest goal for this book was to really help me refine my message and spread it like wildfire.*

I didn't have a business before I wrote this book. I had a blog about children's literature, then I had a method I came up with and I wrote the book about that method.

The feedback from my book has completely led the path for how my business has grown - parents read the book and then said "okay how do I start? What books do I find?" and my business now answers those questions and helps them along their journey.

Sam's advice: Set aside funds to invest in everything that goes into the book so you don't have to do things DIY that aren't your strength. Focus on the writing, make the content amazing.

If you don't have a business yet - really consider why you want to write a book. Do you think a book is absolutely necessary or are there other forms of content you could create? If you decide the book IS what you want, again, invest. This is your first impression on the world!

PUBLISHING STORY

Sam's book IS the cornerstone of her business. It teaches the main principles, pillars, and method upon which all of her other content is built. In order for people to truly understand what she teaches them in my business, she always recommend they read her short, actionable book.

The gives parents a reason to "buy in" to the idea of *The Intentional Bookshelf* and all the value it can bring to their family. Sam enjoys the fact that parents read the book and love the concept and then the next logical step is to join her book club to reap more benefits.

Sam was able to publish quickly. She started the process in September 2016 and published in December 2016. Money was her biggest concern because it was her first real big investment into anything she had ever worked on like this.

She realized she was worth it, that she had a good idea and if she wanted to really make this book happen, she had to invest in that dream.

Sam is not the only one who has launched a business from her book. We talked about how Dana Malstaff's business shifted from her original business coaching idea to one centered on moms after she started writing her book. And then there are "accidental" entrepreneurs, like me, who wrote a book for a passion project that had nothing to do with anything business related, and a business grew out of it. I fell in love with the publishing process when I wrote my book, and decided to figure out how to create a business in author coaching and publishing. And it worked. Another very similar story is our next case study, Maria Dismondy. She felt passionate about writing a children's book and would eventually decide to launch her own publishing company for children's books, Cardinal Press.

"I Decided to Switch Careers" Writer

maria dismondy

AUTHOR & PUBLISHER

"I never planned on leaving my teaching career to build my publishing company."

Maria inspires lives through her poignant stories about topics challenging today's modern child. Maria's background in early education and commitment to teach the importance of character building enables her to touch lives the world over while touring as a public speaker in schools, community forums, and at national conferences. Maria holds a BA and MA in Education and Curriculum and Research from Michigan State University.

I am only one, but still I am one. I cannot do everything, but still I can do something; and because I cannot do everything, I will not refuse to do something that I can do.
~ Edward Everett Hale

www.facebook.com/cardinalrulepress
www.mariadismondy.com

My first book helped establish me as an author and an expert when it comes to educating our children with character. I never planned on leaving my teaching career to build my publishing company. My business started growing when my family started to expand as well.

Maria's advice: Get going TODAY. What are you waiting for? Honestly, there are so many "what ifs" that can hold you back and they will if you let them. Ask yourself the question, Why am I doing this? Find the passion and the purpose in your work and your writing with be authentic.

PUBLISHING STORY

Maria's first book, *Spaghetti In A Hot Dog Bun*, was written because she wanted to share the important message with children that you get to be yourself, no matter what other people say. Her biggest goal was to empower children.

The investment was scary for Maria, especially because during that particular time in their lives they were building a house, just starting out investing their savings and Maria was not making a ton of money as a teacher.

But the investment paid off. Her first book has sold over 250K copies and is now a children's musical that tours the country!

smart positioning

How to Get Your Book Out There

We are not going to spend a large chunk of time on marketing in this book (stay tuned for the next book!) but I did want to cover how you can actually start positioning yourself before you've even completed (or started!) your book.

You can never start marketing your book soon enough. It takes time and effort to grow a large base to sell your books to. You'll want to make sure you're active on social media, you're blogging and bringing people to your website, and you've got some kind of an opt-in or lead magnet (ie, something people will give you their email address to get their hands on!) so that you an further develop this relationship prior to selling your book. You'll also want to seek opportunities to guest post on other blogs, appear on podcasts, participate in online summits and conferences - all in an effort to position yourself as an expert and to bring new fans to you. This way, when it's time to launch your book, you've got a market of eager people waiting to buy the book.

"Pre-Release Activities for Best Sellers" Writer

rachel thompson

AUTHOR & BOOK MARKETING EXPERT

"I learned how to brand myself, what pre-release activities work prior to book launch, all about Amazon, and what it takes to make my five books Number One bestsellers!"

Rachel graduated from California State University, Sacramento in 1986 with a degree in Communications Studies and a Minor in Journalism, and went straight into...selling! After 17+ years in soul-sucking Big Pharma she started her blog, RachelintheOC. She now utilizes her almost two decades of sales, marketing, and training, plus her own experiences in social media and publishing, to helps other authors successful market their books and grow their social media platforms.

No one can make you feel inferior without your consent
~ Eleanor Roosevelt

www.facebook.com/badredheadmedia
www.badredheadmedia.com

I've self-published, hybrid, and traditional. I prefer self-pub because that's how I've made the most money and have the most control. And publishing houses don't do EVERYTHING. That's a fallacy. You still have to do all your own marketing.

My advice: Learn about the publishing industry. Understand that it's a business focused on what will sell. Being an author is owning a business -- you will pay taxes on royalties. Have realistic expectations -- one book will not get you on Oprah's sofa. Book marketing is required. If you can't or won't do it yourself, hire someone to do it for you. Nobody buys a book they've never heard of. Expect to spend money on advertising, marketing, and promotion. Blogging is a must!

Also, having a virtual assistant isn't a luxury -- delegate what you can so you can focus on the writing. Most are very affordable.

PUBLISHING STORY

Rachel's been writing since she was ten-years-old and published her first book in 2011, and her fifth book in 2016.

She had massive success in her pre-marketing efforts. She created the Book Marketing Challenge to help writers figure out how to navigate creating an author platform, across social media, blogging, pre-marketing, and book marketing. Each day she gave them assignments in bite-size chunks so it was very doable and she didn't lose people who felt overwhelmed. The book legitimizes her knowledge and expertise because she's truly been there and done that.

Before she even launched the book, she did massive pre-marketing in two ways: she sent the challenge out free only to people who signed up via newsletter. Over one-thousand people signed up, which gave her enormous beta feedback to improve the book overall. Second, she started #BookMarketingChat (a weekly Twitter chat every Wednesday, 6pm pst/9pm est) which is still going. This also helps her continue to understand what writers struggle with and how she can help them.

self-care

I COMMIT TO TAKING CARE OF ME.

If you're already a busy woman - working your business, maybe raising your family, it's going to take a huge effort to also fit in writing a book. The best way to move forward without burning out is a healthy self-care plan. It doesn't have to be anything major, it can be three minutes of gratitude statements or affirmations before you start working. But make it a priority. It's important.

One Self-Care Ritual You Will Do Every Single Day

____

____

____

____

Sign below:

____

If you miss a day - No big deal! Make it up the next day by doing it twice! If you miss more than 3 in a row, use the next few pages to re-commit.

IT HAPPENS, STICK WITH IT.

Skipped 3 days in a row? It happens. Just re-commit below.

But first, journal (without making excuses) why you think it happened, and what you can do differently moving forward. Change the self-care ritual if it doesn't feel right. It should make you feel good about yourself. It should help you move forward with your writing.

One Self-Care Ritual You Will Do Every Single Day

Sign below:

SELF-CARE FOCUSED WRITER

marietta goldman

HOLISTIC HEALTH COACH

Marietta is a cancer survivor, holistic health coach and self-care advocate who is passionate about helping women naturally heal form the inside out. She believes that True Healing will occur when we can find the balance between healing our physical, mental, emotional and spiritual bodies. She hopes to help women we are stuck in illness make a shift so they can release their fears, open their hearts, trust their intuition and relax into better health. She loves to dance Qoya, practice mindfulness, read, shop, witness the magic of the Universe and spend time with her family. She lives in Midlothian, VA with her husband, three children and their 11 pound puppy.

The soul always knows what to do to heal itself. The challenge is to silence the mind. - Caroline Myss

www.facebook.com/mariettagoldmangroup
www.MariettaGoldman.com

Going through the process of creating and writing a journal was a huge step for me. I knew a journal would be more about the layout and less about the writing but it was a great way for me to build some confidence and become a published author. Creating Positively Intentional *was the catalyst I needed to Ditch the Fear and begin writing a more personal memoir about how cancer and years of emotional eating taught me to lead with my heart, connect with my soul and trust my inner wisdom. What a gift. Thank you to Alexa for giving me the tools and the space and the strength to embrace my vulnerability and begin writing my story without the fear.*

Marietta's advice: You got this! As women sometimes we stand in our own way. Take a deep breathe, let your creative juices flow, trust yourself and don't be afraid to ask for help and guidance from someone who knows the process. Be sure to take care of yourself as well.

PUBLISHING STORY

Marietta's first book, *Positively Intentional: A Journal for Rocking the Anchored Living Lifestyle,* was to offer a hands on journal that women could use to begin getting intentional about the things that might be keeping them stuck in illness. She knew that if women saw a visual about how important it was to tap into their true essence and then assess how key areas in their life were working, they could begin to move forward towards a life with greater health, happiness and connection.

Maritetta believes the journal has been a great activity to get the ball rolling for women who want to explore more about who they really are. For many, the journal is used in conjunction with one-on-one coaching to help women figure out which areas in their life that they need some extra love and attention.

Marietta was completely unaware of how being a published author would impact her marketing, her confidence and even my credibility as a health coach. She knew that once women would love working with the journal, and would then want to work with her more.

Gratitude
IS A POWERFUL THING

Sometimes when you're struggling or working on something that seems really difficult to accomplish, it helps to do gratitude exercises. I'm grateful knowing that you are reading this book and my hard work is paying off. If you have a tough week, take time to remember something you are grateful for with respect to your book. Maybe it's your team, your family for supporting you, and so on.

WEEK1 ______________________________

WEEK2 ______________________________

WEEK3 ______________________________

WEEK4 ______________________________

WEEK5 ______________________________

WEEK6____

WEEK7____

WEEK8 ____

WEEK9 ____

WEEK10____

WEEK11____

WEEK12____

Did you ever consider your book could be something you do in gratitude to your clients?

"Gratitude to my Community" Writer

julie ball
SUBSCRIPTION BOX OWNER

"My biggest goal was to give my subscribers a voice! Each month, Sparkle Hustle Grow includes a book - either for personal development or business growth. I wanted to include my own book, written in part by subscribers, in our 1 year anniversary box."

After running a successful website design & development firm (Grow Web Marketing), Julie wanted to get out from behind the screen. This desire coupled with her biggest inspiration, the female entrepreneur community, is what led her to start Sparkle Hustle Grow, a monthly subscription box for female entrepreneurs. Although a Pittsburgh area native, Julie now lives in Black Mountain, in Western North Carolina.

The more you thank life, the more life gives you to be thankful for. ~ unknown

www.facebook.com/sparklehustlegrow
www.sparklehustlegrow.com

I didn't realize it when I set out to write the book, but being published gives you an opportunity to touch so many people! I have friends, family, and subscribers that are very excited to read it. Interestingly enough, I received several interview requests within days of announcing the book, so I decided to sign up for a local public speaking workshop - which surprised even me!

Julie's advice: I would create a marketing strategy for launch if I did it again. I had a primary purpose of including my book in my monthly subscription boxes, but I discounted all of the other ways I could use the book. I am planning out some launch ideas now, but it would have been a stronger launch had I actually thought "outside of the box."

PUBLISHING STORY

Julie runs a fast-paced business and has less time than ever for "office hours". While she knew that finding the time to write a book would be difficult, she also was committed to doing something special for her subscription box members by writing a book just for them. She decided to join a 30-day book planning group which helped her with mindset and creating deadlines. She hired an editor, who then also became her accountability partner. She credits the completion of her book to this partnership.

Planning
THE KEY TO YOUR SUCCESS

You can have all the dreams int he world, but if you don't set out a plan to help you accomplish them, you are unlikely to see progress.

The following section of the book is a place for you to use to create and stick to a plan for the 90 days, or however long it takes you. Each week you have a space to craft your goals for the week, followed by pages for daily writer affirmations. Why? As we discussed early on, mindset is a huge element of your success, or failure, with a book. Take the time to write a daily affirmation - you don't have to create a new one each day. This can be as simple as "I am a writer and people need my book!" Then set your action steps for writing that day.

SUNDAY, WEEK OF __/__/____

Set aside at least 20 minutes each Sunday to set yourself up for the week ahead. Refer back to the weekly goals and fill them in your first weeks goal here. Specifically, when will you be writing?

My goal for the week is:

____

____

____

What is holding me back?
I release my fears, doubts, & internal talk here.

____

____

On a scale of 1-10, how committed am I to achieving this one goal this week?

1 2 3 4 5 6 7 8 9 10

Other chores, responsibilities, events or distractions this week that I expel now? #no-excuses

____

____

____

2

____________________MONTH ___________/____

I CAN TOTALLY SMASH THIS.

MY WRITER AFFIRMATION FOR TODAY IS:

____

____

TODAY'S 3 ACTION STEPS TO ACHIEVE MY WEEKLY GOAL:

____

____

____

3

MONTH ___________/____

I'M GONNA WIN OVER THIS.

MY WRITER AFFIRMATION FOR TODAY IS:

____

____

TODAY'S 3 ACTION STEPS TO ACHIEVE MY WEEKLY GOAL:

____

____

____

4

MONTH ______________/____

THIS IS WHAT I'M DOING.

MY WRITER AFFIRMATION FOR TODAY IS:

____

____

TODAY'S 3 ACTION STEPS TO ACHIEVE MY WEEKLY GOAL:

____

____

____

5

MONTH ______________/____

IT'S OK TO CATCH UP IF I GET BEHIND.

MY WRITER AFFIRMATION FOR TODAY IS:

____

____

TODAY'S 3 ACTION STEPS TO ACHIEVE MY WEEKLY GOAL:

____

____

MONTH ____________/____

WRAP THIS BABY UP.

6

MY WRITER AFFIRMATION FOR TODAY IS:

____

____

TODAY'S 3 ACTION STEPS TO ACHIEVE MY WEEKLY GOAL:

____

____

____

7

MONTH ____________/____

REFLECT & REWARD

MY WRITER AFFIRMATION FOR TODAY IS:

____

____

TODAY'S 3 ACTION STEPS TO ACHIEVE MY WEEKLY GOAL:

____

____

____

9

MONTH _______________/_____

I CAN TOTALLY SMASH THIS.

MY WRITER AFFIRMATION FOR TODAY IS:

___

___

TODAY'S 3 ACTION STEPS TO ACHIEVE MY WEEKLY GOAL:

___

___

___

10

MONTH _______________/_____

I'M GONNA WIN OVER THIS.

MY WRITER AFFIRMATION FOR TODAY IS:

___

___

TODAY'S 3 ACTION STEPS TO ACHIEVE MY WEEKLY GOAL:

___

___

___

11

MONTH ______________/____

THIS IS WHAT I'M DOING.

MY WRITER AFFIRMATION FOR TODAY IS:

____

____

TODAY'S 3 ACTION STEPS TO ACHIEVE MY WEEKLY GOAL:

____

____

____

12

MONTH ______________/____

IT'S OK TO CATCH UP IF I GET BEHIND.

MY WRITER AFFIRMATION FOR TODAY IS:

____

____

TODAY'S 3 ACTION STEPS TO ACHIEVE MY WEEKLY GOAL:

13

MONTH ____________/____

WRAP THIS BABY UP.

MY WRITER AFFIRMATION FOR TODAY IS:

____

____

TODAY'S 3 ACTION STEPS TO ACHIEVE MY WEEKLY GOAL:

____

____

____

14

MONTH ____________/____

REFLECT & REWARD

MY WRITER AFFIRMATION FOR TODAY IS:

____

____

TODAY'S 3 ACTION STEPS TO ACHIEVE MY WEEKLY GOAL:

SUNDAY, WEEK OF __/__/____

Set aside at least 20 minutes each Sunday to set yourself up for the week ahead. Refer back to the weekly goals and fill them in your first weeks goal here. Specifically, when will you be writing?

My goal for the week is:

____

____

____

What is holding me back?
I release my fears, doubts, & internal talk here.

____

____

On a scale of 1-10, how committed am I to achieving this one goal this week?

1 2 3 4 5 6 7 8 9 10

Other chores, responsibilities, events or distractions this week that I expel now? #noexcuses

____

____

16

MONTH ____________/____

I CAN TOTALLY SMASH THIS.

MY WRITER AFFIRMATION FOR TODAY IS:

____

____

TODAY'S 3 ACTION STEPS TO ACHIEVE MY WEEKLY GOAL:

____

____

____

17

MONTH ____________/____

I'M GONNA WIN OVER THIS.

MY WRITER AFFIRMATION FOR TODAY IS:

____

____

TODAY'S 3 ACTION STEPS TO ACHIEVE MY WEEKLY GOAL:

18

MONTH ____________/____

THIS IS WHAT I'M DOING.

MY WRITER AFFIRMATION FOR TODAY IS:

____

____

TODAY'S 3 ACTION STEPS TO ACHIEVE MY WEEKLY GOAL:

____

____

____

19

MONTH ____________/____

IT'S OK TO CATCH UP IF I GET BEHIND.

MY WRITER AFFIRMATION FOR TODAY IS:

____

____

TODAY'S 3 ACTION STEPS TO ACHIEVE MY WEEKLY GOAL:

20

MONTH ____________/____

WRAP THIS BABY UP.

MY WRITER AFFIRMATION FOR TODAY IS:

____

____

TODAY'S 3 ACTION STEPS TO ACHIEVE MY WEEKLY GOAL:

____

____

____

21

MONTH ____________/____

REFLECT & REWARD

MY WRITER AFFIRMATION FOR TODAY IS:

____

____

TODAY'S 3 ACTION STEPS TO ACHIEVE MY WEEKLY GOAL:

Week 4: Day 22

SUNDAY, WEEK OF __/__/____

Set aside at least 20 minutes each Sunday to set yourself up for the week ahead. Refer back to the weekly goals and fill them in your first weeks goal here. Specifically, when will you be writing?

My goal for the week is:

___

___

___

What is holding me back?
I release my fears, doubts, & internal talk here.

___

___

On a scale of 1-10, how committed am I to achieving this one goal this week?

1 2 3 4 5 6 7 8 9 10

Other chores, responsibilities, events or distractions this week that I expel now? #noexcuses

___

___

MONTH ____________/____

I CAN TOTALLY SMASH THIS.

23

MY WRITER AFFIRMATION FOR TODAY IS:

____

____

TODAY'S 3 ACTION STEPS TO ACHIEVE MY WEEKLY GOAL:

____

____

____

MONTH ____________/____

I'M GONNA WIN OVER THIS.

24

MY WRITER AFFIRMATION FOR TODAY IS:

____

____

TODAY'S 3 ACTION STEPS TO ACHIEVE MY WEEKLY GOAL:

25

MONTH ____________/____

THIS IS WHAT I'M DOING.

MY WRITER AFFIRMATION FOR TODAY IS:

____

____

TODAY'S 3 ACTION STEPS TO ACHIEVE MY WEEKLY GOAL:

____

____

____

26

MONTH ____________/____

IT'S OK TO CATCH UP IF I GET BEHIND.

MY WRITER AFFIRMATION FOR TODAY IS:

____

____

TODAY'S 3 ACTION STEPS TO ACHIEVE MY WEEKLY GOAL:

____

____

MONTH ____________/____

WRAP THIS BABY UP.

27

MY WRITER AFFIRMATION FOR TODAY IS:

____

____

TODAY'S 3 ACTION STEPS TO ACHIEVE MY WEEKLY GOAL:

____

____

____

MONTH ____________/____

REFLECT & REWARD

28

MY WRITER AFFIRMATION FOR TODAY IS:

____

____

TODAY'S 3 ACTION STEPS TO ACHIEVE MY WEEKLY GOAL:

SUNDAY, WEEK OF __/__/____

Set aside at least 20 minutes each Sunday to set yourself up for the week ahead. Refer back to the weekly goals and fill them in your first weeks goal here. Specifically, when will you be writing?

My goal for the week is:

____

____

____

What is holding me back?
I release my fears, doubts, & internal talk here.

____

____

On a scale of 1-10, how committed am I to achieving this one goal this week?

1 2 3 4 5 6 7 8 9 10

Other chores, responsibilities, events or distractions this week that I expel now? #noexcuses

____

____

____

20

MONTH ____________/____

I CAN TOTALLY SMASH THIS.

TMY WRITER AFFIRMATION FOR TODAY IS:

____

____

TODAY'S 3 ACTION STEPS TO ACHIEVE MY WEEKLY GOAL:

____

____

____

31

MONTH ____________/____

I'M GONNA WIN OVER THIS.

MY WRITER AFFIRMATION FOR TODAY IS:

____

____

TODAY'S 3 ACTION STEPS TO ACHIEVE MY WEEKLY GOAL:

____

____

32

MONTH ____________/____

THIS IS WHAT I'M DOING.

TODAY I AM GRATEFUL FOR:

____

MY ONE DAILY KINDNESS:

____

TODAY'S 3 ACTION STEPS TO ACHIEVE MY WEEKLY GOAL:

____

____

____

33

MONTH ____________/____

IT'S OK TO CATCH UP IF I GET BEHIND.

TODAY I AM GRATEFUL FOR:

____

MY ONE DAILY KINDNESS:

____

TODAY'S 3 ACTION STEPS TO ACHIEVE MY WEEKLY GOAL:

____

____

____

MONTH ____________/____

WRAP THIS BABY UP.

34

TODAY I AM GRATEFUL FOR:

___

MY ONE DAILY KINDNESS:

___

TODAY'S 3 ACTION STEPS TO ACHIEVE MY WEEKLY GOAL:

___

___

___

MONTH ____________/____

REFLECT & REWARD

35

HOW FAR DID I GET AT ACHIEVING MY GOAL?

___

WHAT CAN I DO BETTER NEXT WEEK?

___

I TOTALLY ROCKED IT! TO REWARD MYSELF I WILL. .

___

___

___

Week 6: Day 36

SUNDAY, WEEK OF __/__/____

Set aside at least 20 minutes each Sunday to set yourself up for the week ahead. Refer back to the weekly goals and fill them in your first weeks goal here. Specifically, when will you be writing?

My goal for the week is:

___

___

___

What is holding me back?
I release my fears, doubts, & internal talk here.

___

___

On a scale of 1-10, how committed am I to achieving this one goal this week?

1 2 3 4 5 6 7 8 9 10

Other chores, responsibilities, events or distractions this week that I expel now? #noexcuses

___

___

MONTH ____________/____

I CAN TOTALLY SMASH THIS.

37

MY WRITER AFFIRMATION FOR TODAY IS:

____

____

TODAY'S 3 ACTION STEPS TO ACHIEVE MY WEEKLY GOAL:

____

____

____

MONTH ____________/____

I'M GONNA WIN OVER THIS.

38

MY WRITER AFFIRMATION FOR TODAY IS:

____

____

TODAY'S 3 ACTION STEPS TO ACHIEVE MY WEEKLY GOAL:

39

MONTH ____________/____

THIS IS WHAT I'M DOING.

MY WRITER AFFIRMATION FOR TODAY IS:

____

____

TODAY'S 3 ACTION STEPS TO ACHIEVE MY WEEKLY GOAL:

____

____

____

40

MONTH ____________/____

IT'S OK TO CATCH UP IF I GET BEHIND.

MY WRITER AFFIRMATION FOR TODAY IS:

____

____

TODAY'S 3 ACTION STEPS TO ACHIEVE MY WEEKLY GOAL:

____

____

41

MONTH ___________/___

WRAP THIS BABY UP.

MY WRITER AFFIRMATION FOR TODAY IS:

____

____

TODAY'S 3 ACTION STEPS TO ACHIEVE MY WEEKLY GOAL:

____

____

____

42

MONTH ___________/___

REFLECT & REWARD

MY WRITER AFFIRMATION FOR TODAY IS:

____

____

TODAY'S 3 ACTION STEPS TO ACHIEVE MY WEEKLY GOAL:

almost half-way
CHECK IN

We've made it almost half-way through your journey! How are you doing? Are you hanging in there? Are the daily affirmations helping you?

Here's one more featured author story to help you as you continue on. Mary Shores never considered herself a writer, but she had a dream and never gave up on it!

mary shores

AUTHOR, SPEAKER, ENTREPRENEUR, & CEO

"I took the barrier belief of I'm not a writer, and I changed it to, how do I become a writer? Which allowed me to begin actually honing my skills and taking the steps necessary to write a book."

Mary Shores teaches individuals and businesses to fearlessly create their own realities by using scientific methods and practical personal development. She is the founder and CEO of a multi-million dollar business, one of the most unique collection agencies in the country. She is the revolutionary founder of the Words That Work system, which inspired her book, Conscious Communications.

Everything you do in life, every choice you make, either creates connection or drives disconnection.

www.facebook.com/shoresmary
www.maryshores.com

WORDS OF WISDOM
MARY SHORES

I always knew I wanted to be a writer, but I repeated this mantra of "I want to write a book but I'm not a writer," so the book just lived inside of me for years. "I'm not a writer is uncovering that deep down inside something needed cleared. I began attending writer's workshops, which helped get my actions in alignment with my dream of writing a book. One of my biggest goals was to be published with my favorite publisher, Hay House, which I accomplished!

Whenever I got writers block I just switched up the chapter I was writing to give my mind a break from thinking too hard on the subject at hand. I also did things to keep my motivation high like personal growth workshops and writing a page of affirmations every day! The result is I have 1,000's of affirmations to share!

Mary's advice - start marketing your book EARLY! Her second piece of advice - Do it! Every person – but female entrepreneurs specifically – has a unique arsenal of experiences, tools, perspectives, and more that can help other people.

I think female entrepreneurs also need to build each other up because it's a hard world out there for businesswomen. Make the right connections, attend writing workshops, and write the damn book.

PUBLISHING STORY

Mary always wanted to be published by Hay House, which she did accomplish. It took a lot of mindset work for her to consider herself a writer. She used to repeat this mantra of *I'm not a writer*, which of course prevented her from following her dream of writing a book. Even when she attended writing conferences, she would sometimes introduce herself and say, "Hi, I'm Mary, I'm not a writer." She was holding myself back because of my limiting mindset. Eventually she worked through this and now definitely considers herself a writer.

It took 2 and a half years to complete *Conscious Communications*. The proposal alone took 7 months to complete, and then she had 9 months to write the manuscript. Editing was an ongoing process over 6 months, and then the book was finally ready for packaging and printing which took another 6 months. Be prepared for a lengthy process if going the traditional route. Mary said she was surprised that, although her book was published by Hay House, she was in charge of marketing and promoting *Conscious Communications* on my own.

I was so happy and excited and completely ready to go that I didn't really need any help meeting deadlines.

SUNDAY, WEEK OF __/__/____

Set aside at least 20 minutes each Sunday to set yourself up for the week ahead. Refer back to the weekly goals and fill them in your first weeks goal here. Specifically, when will you be writing?

My goal for the week is:

____

____

____

What is holding me back?
I release my fears, doubts, & internal talk here.

____

____

On a scale of 1-10, how committed am I to achieving this one goal this week?

1 2 3 4 5 6 7 8 9 10

Other chores, responsibilities, events or distractions this week that I expel now? #noexcuses

____

____

MONTH ______________/____

I CAN TOTALLY SMASH THIS.

44

MY WRITER AFFIRMATION FOR TODAY IS:

____

____

TODAY'S 3 ACTION STEPS TO ACHIEVE MY WEEKLY GOAL:

____

____

____

MONTH ______________/____

I'M GONNA WIN OVER THIS.

45

MY WRITER AFFIRMATION FOR TODAY IS:

____

____

TODAY'S 3 ACTION STEPS TO ACHIEVE MY WEEKLY GOAL:

46

MONTH ______________/____

THIS IS WHAT I'M DOING.

MY WRITER AFFIRMATION FOR TODAY IS:

___

___

TODAY'S 3 ACTION STEPS TO ACHIEVE MY WEEKLY GOAL:

___

___

___

47

MONTH ______________/____

IT'S OK TO CATCH UP IF I GET BEHIND.

MY WRITER AFFIRMATION FOR TODAY IS:

___

___

TODAY'S 3 ACTION STEPS TO ACHIEVE MY WEEKLY GOAL:

___

48

MONTH ______________/____

WRAP THIS BABY UP.

MY WRITER AFFIRMATION FOR TODAY IS:

____

____

TODAY'S 3 ACTION STEPS TO ACHIEVE MY WEEKLY GOAL:

____

____

____

49

MONTH ______________/____

REFLECT & REWARD

MY WRITER AFFIRMATION FOR TODAY IS:

____

____

TODAY'S 3 ACTION STEPS TO ACHIEVE MY WEEKLY GOAL:

____

____

SUNDAY, WEEK OF __/__/____

Set aside at least 20 minutes each Sunday to set yourself up for the week ahead. Refer back to the weekly goals and fill them in your first weeks goal here. Specifically, when will you be writing?

My goal for the week is:

____

____

____

What is holding me back?
I release my fears, doubts, & internal talk here.

____

____

On a scale of 1-10, how committed am I to achieving this one goal this week?

1 2 3 4 5 6 7 8 9 10

Other chores, responsibilities, events or distractions this week that I expel now? #noexcuses

____

____

MONTH ____________/____

I CAN TOTALLY SMASH THIS.

51

TODAY I AM GRATEFUL FOR:

____

MY ONE DAILY KINDNESS:

____

TODAY'S 3 ACTION STEPS TO ACHIEVE MY WEEKLY GOAL:

____

____

____

MONTH ____________/____

I'M GONNA WIN OVER THIS.

52

TODAY I AM GRATEFUL FOR:

____

MY ONE DAILY KINDNESS:

____

TODAY'S 3 ACTION STEPS TO ACHIEVE MY WEEKLY GOAL:

____

____

____

53

MONTH ____________/____

THIS IS WHAT I'M DOING.

MY WRITER AFFIRMATION FOR TODAY IS:

____

____

TODAY'S 3 ACTION STEPS TO ACHIEVE MY WEEKLY GOAL:

____

____

____

54

MONTH ____________/____

IT'S OK TO CATCH UP IF I GET BEHIND.

MY WRITER AFFIRMATION FOR TODAY IS:

____

____

TODAY'S 3 ACTION STEPS TO ACHIEVE MY WEEKLY GOAL:

____

____

MONTH ____________/____

WRAP THIS BABY UP.

55

MY WRITER AFFIRMATION FOR TODAY IS:

____

____

TODAY'S 3 ACTION STEPS TO ACHIEVE MY WEEKLY GOAL:

____

____

____

MONTH ____________/____

REFLECT & REWARD

56

MY WRITER AFFIRMATION FOR TODAY IS:

____

____

TODAY'S 3 ACTION STEPS TO ACHIEVE MY WEEKLY GOAL:

____

____

____

SUNDAY, WEEK OF __/__/____

Set aside at least 20 minutes each Sunday to set yourself up for the week ahead. Refer back to the weekly goals and fill them in your first weeks goal here. Specifically, when will you be writing?

My goal for the week is:

___

___

___

What is holding me back?
I release my fears, doubts, & internal talk here.

___

___

On a scale of 1-10, how committed am I to achieving this one goal this week?

1 2 3 4 5 6 7 8 9 10

Other chores, responsibilities, events or distractions this week that I expel now? #noexcuses

___

___

58

MONTH ____________/____

I CAN TOTALLY SMASH THIS.

MY WRITER AFFIRMATION FOR TODAY IS:

____

____

TODAY'S 3 ACTION STEPS TO ACHIEVE MY WEEKLY GOAL:

____

____

____

59

MONTH ____________/____

I'M GONNA WIN OVER THIS.

MY WRITER AFFIRMATION FOR TODAY IS:

____

____

TODAY'S 3 ACTION STEPS TO ACHIEVE MY WEEKLY GOAL:

60

MONTH ____________/____

THIS IS WHAT I'M DOING.

MY WRITER AFFIRMATION FOR TODAY IS:

____

____

TODAY'S 3 ACTION STEPS TO ACHIEVE MY WEEKLY GOAL:

____

____

____

61

MONTH ____________/____

IT'S OK TO CATCH UP IF I GET BEHIND.

MY WRITER AFFIRMATION FOR TODAY IS:

____

____

TODAY'S 3 ACTION STEPS TO ACHIEVE MY WEEKLY GOAL:

____

____

MONTH ____________/____

WRAP THIS BABY UP.

62

MY WRITER AFFIRMATION FOR TODAY IS:

____

____

TODAY'S 3 ACTION STEPS TO ACHIEVE MY WEEKLY GOAL:

____

____

____

MONTH ____________/____

REFLECT & REWARD

63

MY WRITER AFFIRMATION FOR TODAY IS:

____

____

TODAY'S 3 ACTION STEPS TO ACHIEVE MY WEEKLY GOAL:

____

____

____

SUNDAY, WEEK OF __/__/____

Set aside at least 20 minutes each Sunday to set yourself up for the week ahead. Refer back to the weekly goals and fill them in your first weeks goal here. Specifically, when will you be writing?

My goal for the week is:

____

____

____

What is holding me back?
I release my fears, doubts, & internal talk here.

____

____

On a scale of 1-10, how committed am I to achieving this one goal this week?

1 2 3 4 5 6 7 8 9 10

Other chores, responsibilities, events or distractions this week that I expel now? #noexcuses

____

____

65

MONTH ____________/____

I CAN TOTALLY SMASH THIS.

MY WRITER AFFIRMATION FOR TODAY IS:

____

____

TODAY'S 3 ACTION STEPS TO ACHIEVE MY WEEKLY GOAL:

____

____

____

66

MONTH ____________/____

I'M GONNA WIN OVER THIS.

MY WRITER AFFIRMATION FOR TODAY IS:

____

____

TODAY'S 3 ACTION STEPS TO ACHIEVE MY WEEKLY GOAL:

67

MONTH ____________/____

THIS IS WHAT I'M DOING.

MY WRITER AFFIRMATION FOR TODAY IS:

____

____

TODAY'S 3 ACTION STEPS TO ACHIEVE MY WEEKLY GOAL:

____

____

____

68

MONTH ____________/____

IT'S OK TO CATCH UP IF I GET BEHIND.

MY WRITER AFFIRMATION FOR TODAY IS:

____

____

TODAY'S 3 ACTION STEPS TO ACHIEVE MY WEEKLY GOAL:

____

____

69

MONTH ______________/____

WRAP THIS BABY UP.

MY WRITER AFFIRMATION FOR TODAY IS:

___

___

TODAY'S 3 ACTION STEPS TO ACHIEVE MY WEEKLY GOAL:

___

___

___

70

MONTH ______________/____

REFLECT & REWARD

MY WRITER AFFIRMATION FOR TODAY IS:

___

___

TODAY'S 3 ACTION STEPS TO ACHIEVE MY WEEKLY GOAL:

SUNDAY, WEEK OF __/__/____

Set aside at least 20 minutes each Sunday to set yourself up for the week ahead. Refer back to the weekly goals and fill them in your first weeks goal here. Specifically, when will you be writing?

My goal for the week is:

____

____

____

What is holding me back?
I release my fears, doubts, & internal talk here.

____

____

On a scale of 1-10, how committed am I to achieving this one goal this week?

1 2 3 4 5 6 7 8 9 10

Other chores, responsibilities, events or distractions this week that I expel now? #noexcuses

____

____

72

MONTH ____________/____

I CAN TOTALLY SMASH THIS.

MY WRITER AFFIRMATION FOR TODAY IS:

____

____

TODAY'S 3 ACTION STEPS TO ACHIEVE MY WEEKLY GOAL:

____

____

____

73

MONTH ____________/____

I'M GONNA WIN OVER THIS.

MY WRITER AFFIRMATION FOR TODAY IS:

____

____

TODAY'S 3 ACTION STEPS TO ACHIEVE MY WEEKLY GOAL:

74

MONTH ______________/____

THIS IS WHAT I'M DOING.

MY WRITER AFFIRMATION FOR TODAY IS:

____

____

TODAY'S 3 ACTION STEPS TO ACHIEVE MY WEEKLY GOAL:

____

____

____

75

MONTH ______________/____

IT'S OK TO CATCH UP IF I GET BEHIND.

MY WRITER AFFIRMATION FOR TODAY IS:

____

____

TODAY'S 3 ACTION STEPS TO ACHIEVE MY WEEKLY GOAL:

76

MONTH ____________/____

WRAP THIS BABY UP.

MY WRITER AFFIRMATION FOR TODAY IS:

____

____

TODAY'S 3 ACTION STEPS TO ACHIEVE MY WEEKLY GOAL:

____

____

____

77

MONTH ____________/____

REFLECT & REWARD

MY WRITER AFFIRMATION FOR TODAY IS:

____

____

TODAY'S 3 ACTION STEPS TO ACHIEVE MY WEEKLY GOAL:

____

____

____

SUNDAY, WEEK OF __/__/____

Set aside at least 20 minutes each Sunday to set yourself up for the week ahead. Refer back to the weekly goals and fill them in your first weeks goal here. Specifically, when will you be writing?

My goal for the week is:

____

____

____

What is holding me back?
I release my fears, doubts, & internal talk here.

____

____

On a scale of 1-10, how committed am I to achieving this one goal this week?

1 2 3 4 5 6 7 8 9 10

Other chores, responsibilities, events or distractions this week that I expel now? #noexcuses

____

____

79

MONTH ____________/____

I CAN TOTALLY SMASH THIS.

MY WRITER AFFIRMATION FOR TODAY IS:

____

____

TODAY'S 3 ACTION STEPS TO ACHIEVE MY WEEKLY GOAL:

____

____

____

80

MONTH ____________/____

I'M GONNA WIN OVER THIS.

MY WRITER AFFIRMATION FOR TODAY IS:

____

____

TODAY'S 3 ACTION STEPS TO ACHIEVE MY WEEKLY GOAL:

____

____

____

81

MONTH ______________/____

THIS IS WHAT I'M DOING.

MY WRITER AFFIRMATION FOR TODAY IS:

____

____

TODAY'S 3 ACTION STEPS TO ACHIEVE MY WEEKLY GOAL:

____

____

____

82

MONTH ______________/____

IT'S OK TO CATCH UP IF I GET BEHIND.

MY WRITER AFFIRMATION FOR TODAY IS:

____

____

TODAY'S 3 ACTION STEPS TO ACHIEVE MY WEEKLY GOAL:

____

____

____

83

MONTH ___________/____

WRAP THIS BABY UP.

MY WRITER AFFIRMATION FOR TODAY IS:

____

____

TODAY'S 3 ACTION STEPS TO ACHIEVE MY WEEKLY GOAL:

____

____

____

84

MONTH ___________/____

REFLECT & REWARD

MY WRITER AFFIRMATION FOR TODAY IS:

____

____

TODAY'S 3 ACTION STEPS TO ACHIEVE MY WEEKLY GOAL:

____

____

____

rebecca undem

BLOGGER, AUTHOR, SPEAKER, COACH

"Not everyone has a book on their heart and I believe those that do have almost an obligation to get it from their heart to paper."

Rebecca Undem yearns to live in a world with bold, inspired people who aren't afraid of making mistakes; with a forever-full cup of coffee in her hand, preferably nut-flavored. She is the author of the book *How Mommy Got Her Groove Back*.

No one can make you feel inferior without your consent.- Eleanor Roosevelt

www.facebook.com/rebeccaundem
www.rebeccaundem.com

My book is a personal memoir so literally, if you want to understand me better, you can read my book, and you'll know! I had a lot of fears about sharing personal stories, especially my mothers. She's extremely private and I'm more of an open book. When she told me I could publish what I'd written, I asked her why she was OK with it all and she replied with, "Maybe this story will help someone else." It was a perfect reminder to me that all stories matter. As for the money fear, I knew that I'd never be satisfied until I finished it so if I wanted a book to be a part of my offering, I'd have to just bite the bullet and make it happen.

Rebeca's advice: Like the title of this book says, Just Write It! So many women I meet have a book on their hearts and whether you want to sell a ton of copies and make a real business from your book or you just want to get your story down on paper, you must start!

PUBLISHING STORY

After blogging for a couple of years, writing a book seemed like the natural next step for Rebecca. She says it had always been a goal of hers anyway. She wanted to connect with other women who felt the same struggles that she did.

Originally, Rebecca had no intention of writing a memoir. She had actually written an entirely different manuscript based more on the writing from her blog but when her editor took a pass through the first 29 pages, she encouraged her to start from scratch and tell her story. Rebecca says her scared inner critic immediately chimed in with, "Why would anyone care about your story? You're from a small town in North Dakota. Why would that matter?" Also Rebecca was worried about the associated costs with writing a book. But, she's glad she made the leap of faith.

She feels her book has created a very obvious way for people to determine who she really is as a coach. Rebecca had some concerns about sharing personal stories of people she loves in her book, particularly was about sharing my mother's part of the story, but getting her blessing to write her part of our story is what allowed her to move past her own worthiness fears.

In the future, she likes the thought of trying to be published through a traditional house.

The Way to Get Started
Is To Quit Talking And
Begin Doing.

-Walt Disney

Week 13: Day 85

SUNDAY, WEEK OF __/__/____

Set aside at least 20 minutes each Sunday to set yourself up for the week ahead. Refer back to the weekly goals and fill them in your first weeks goal here. Specifically, when will you be writing?

My goal for the week is:

____

____

____

What is holding me back?
I release my fears, doubts, & internal talk here.

____

____

On a scale of 1-10, how committed am I to achieving this one goal this week?

1 2 3 4 5 6 7 8 9 10

Other chores, responsibilities, events or distractions this week that I expel now? #noexcuses

____

____

86

MONTH ____________/____

I CAN TOTALLY SMASH THIS.

MY WRITER AFFIRMATION FOR TODAY IS:

____

____

TODAY'S 3 ACTION STEPS TO ACHIEVE MY WEEKLY GOAL:

____

____

____

87

MONTH ____________/____

I'M GONNA WIN OVER THIS.

MY WRITER AFFIRMATION FOR TODAY IS:

____

____

TODAY'S 3 ACTION STEPS TO ACHIEVE MY WEEKLY GOAL:

88

MONTH ______________/____

THIS IS WHAT I'M DOING.

MY WRITER AFFIRMATION FOR TODAY IS:

____

____

TODAY'S 3 ACTION STEPS TO ACHIEVE MY WEEKLY GOAL:

____

____

____

89

MONTH ______________/____

IT'S OK TO CATCH UP IF I GET BEHIND.

MY WRITER AFFIRMATION FOR TODAY IS:

____

____

TODAY'S 3 ACTION STEPS TO ACHIEVE MY WEEKLY GOAL:

____

____

____

MONTH ___________/____

WRAP THIS BABY UP.

90

MY WRITER AFFIRMATION FOR TODAY IS:

____

____

TODAY'S 3 ACTION STEPS TO ACHIEVE MY WEEKLY GOAL:

____

____

____

rocked that!

NOW THAT'S HOW IT'S DONE.

DID I ACHIEVE MY GOAL?

____

____

HOW DOES IT FEEL TO FINISH?

____

____

____

AUTHOR

alexa bigwarfe

Alexa Bigwarfe is a mother to 3 wildlings, author, publisher, writer-entrepreneur, and podcaster. Her writing career began after her infant daughter passed away at 2 days old. She has written and/or edited and self-published numerous books of her own and for other authors through her hybrid publishing company, Kat Biggie Press. She uses that hard-earned publishing knowledge to support other writers and small businesses in completing, publishing, and marketing their books through her company Write. Publish.Sell. (http://writepublishsell.co) Join her free group about writing and publishing at http://facebook.com/groups/WritePublishSell.

www.writepublishsell.co
www.katbiggiepress.com

NOW WHAT?

Congratulations on making it through the journal!
By the end of 90 days, hopefully you've made some great progress in your book. If you need some extra help in moving forward, finishing the book, and preparing it for publication, I would love to work with you. I offer several different levels of coaching, a la carte services, and my Write | Publish | Sell Academy to move you through the rest of your book writing, publishing, and marketing journey. Please feel free to reach out to me at info@writepublishsell.co, or check out my website at writepublishsell.co

If you're interested in giving the Academy a whirl, you can try your first month for $1. Head on over to http://writepublishsell.thinkific.com/courses/wps-academy and use the coupon code tryme1 .

I'm so excited that you've started this journey and I cannot wait to see how it goes for you! Please keep me posted!

With Love,

Alexa

THANK YOU

The journal you're holding in your hands is one of the tools in the *Just Write It!* program. I want to say a big thanks to all the people without who helped me bring it to life.

Thank you Neesha Mirchandani for connecting me with Cindy Tyler and Vervante Press. Thank you for bringing us together with this enormous idea and for encouraging me to get to this point. Michelle, your cover design skills never cease to amaze me! Nancy, I couldn't ever ask for a better assistant in running this business. Thank you, truly, for all you do.

Thank you especially to all of the authors who bravely contributed their stories, fears, and publishing successes and challenges. You made this book a real pleasure to write.

Jeff, Braedan, Ella, and Charis... you four sacrificed a lot for this to happen, and you're all a key element of this project.

Alexa Bigwarfe CEO, Write | Publish | Sell

Would You be Interested in a "Quick Win"?

As an author coach, I find that my busiest clients don't have the time to stare at a blank page. It's much easier for them to start from a proven results-based system: it shaves months from the publishing process. I came across a perfect solution so I decided to try it. The book you're holding in your hands is the result.

Just Write It was created by licensing the plug-and-play Quick Wins Productivity System by Impact Stars, LLC.

It is a series of ready-to-go productivity and storytelling templates designed to give readers a victory - within the pages of a book.

Once they taste your brand and your expertise, they can make a decision if they are ready to make a deeper commitment to your brand. If you hate 'pitching', this is a great way to let a product do the selling for you: the proof is in the pudding!

My company, Write.Publish.Sell is certified to customize the Quick Wins System to your needs and make it available on Amazon and other platforms. The template is a great starting point but you will be amazed to see where we take it together.

If you loved the structure of this book, you will love what we create for your brand even more. It is an author concierge experience with a focused business result.

In fact, if you're an action-taker, you could be holding YOUR very own workbook just like this one in your hands, in less than 90 days.

Visit https://impactstars.com/alexa to apply for a license, only limited licenses are issued every month, and only if there is a strategic fit.

What I love best about the Quick Wins System is it includes a partnership with a highly reputed custom printer, Vervante. Once your book is ready, you can sell the book at speaking events and ship the book to high-value clients to make a great first impression with a click of a button. Vervante will also fulfill orders from your website so you don't have to worry about any of those tedious details. And you definitely don't have to wait in line at the post office, because your shipping and handling is all automated, while you focus on growing your business, and writing more books.

If you are a speaker, consultant, coach or entrepreneur, and your sales funnel doesn't have a great entry-level product that converts prospects into buyers while building your brand authority, this may be the right 'first book' for you!

Not sure? Contact me at http://writepublishsell.co/contact/ or info@writepublishsell.co and I will advise you.